# Mistake-Proofing

The Management Master Series

William F. Christopher
Editor-in-Chief

# 11

# Mistake-Proofing

## Designing Errors Out

Richard B. Chase
and
Douglas M. Stewart

PRODUCTIVITY PRESS

Portland, Oregon

Volume 11 of the *Management Master Series*
William F. Christopher, Editor-in-Chief
Copyright © 1995 by Productivity Press, Inc.

Productivity Press
P.O. Box 13390
Portland, OR 97213-0390
United States of America
Telephone: 503-235-0600
Telefax: 503-235-0909

ISBN: 1-56327-076-5

Book and cover design by William Stanton
Cover illustration by Paul Zwolak
Typeset by Laser Words, Madras, India
Printed and bound by BookCrafters in the United States of America

*Library of Congress Cataloging-in-Publication Data*

Chase, Richard B.
    Mistake-proofing: designing errors out / Richard B. Chase and
    Douglas M. Stewart.
        p.    cm. – (Management master series; v. 11)
    1. Management. 2. Errors. I. Stewart, Douglas M. II. Title. III. Series.
    HD38.C43184   1995                                              94-24003
    658.4 – dc20                                                          CIP

00 99 98 97 96 95   10 9 8 7 6 5 4 3 2 1

# — CONTENTS —

Publisher's Message    vii

1. **Introduction    1**
   What Is Mistake-Proofing?    2
   The Idea Behind Mistake-Proofing    5

2. **So Where Do Mistakes Come From?    7**
   Machine Mistakes    7
   Human Mistakes    9

3. **Where and When to Look for Mistakes    17**
   Inspect Close to the Source    17
   General Location Guidelines    18
   Other Critical Inspection Points    20
   Inspect All of the Time    21

4. **Finding the Mistakes    23**
   Self-Monitoring    23
   Checking by Others    24
   Environmental Cues    24
   Detection of Machine Mistakes    28

5. **Poka-Yokes: Devices and Methods for
   Mistake-Proof Operations    29**
   Keep It Simple    30
   Types of Poka-Yokes    32
   Physical Poka-Yokes    32
   Sequencing Poka-Yokes    45

Grouping and Counting Poka-Yokes   50
Information Enhancement Poka-Yokes   54

6. **Designing Out the Mistakes   61**
Process Maps   61
Developing Mistake-Proofing Devices
   or Procedures   65
Other Important Design Issues   66

7. **Summary   70**
Mistake-Proofing Works Best When...   70
Mistake-Proofing and Your Customers   71
Mistake-Proofing and Your Employees   71
How Far Can You Go in Mistake-Proofing?   71

**Notes   73**
**About the Authors   78**

# PUBLISHER'S MESSAGE

The *Management Master Series* was designed to discover and disseminate to you the world's best concepts, principles, and current practices in excellent management. We present this information in a concise and easy-to-use format to provide you with the tools and techniques you need to stay abreast of this rapidly accelerating world of ideas.

World-class competitiveness requires managers today to be thoroughly informed about how and what other internationally successful managers are doing. What works? What doesn't? and Why?

Management is often considered a "neglected art." It is not possible to know how to manage before you are made a manager. But once you become a manager you are expected to know how to manage and to do it well, right from the start.

One result of this neglect in management training has been managers who rely on control rather than creativity. Certainly, managers in this century have shown a distinct neglect of workers as creative human beings. The idea that employees are an organization's most valuable asset is still very new. How managers can inspire and direct the creativity and intelligence of everyone involved in the work of an organization has only begun to emerge.

Perhaps if we consider management as a "science" the task of learning how to manage well will be easier. A scientist begins with an hypothesis and then runs experiments to observe whether the hypothesis is correct. Scientists depend on detailed notes about the experiment—the timing, the ingredients, the amounts—and carefully record all results as they test new hypotheses. Certain things come to be known by this method; for instance, that water always consists of one part oxygen and two parts hydrogen.

We as managers must learn from our experience and from the experience of others. The scientific approach provides a model for learning. Science begins with vision and desired outcomes, and achieves its purpose through observation, experiment, and analysis of precisely recorded results. And then what is newly discovered is shared so that each person's research will build on the work of others.

Our organizations, however, rarely provide the time for learning or experimentation. As a manager, you need information from those who have already experimented and learned and recorded their results. You need it in brief, clear, and detailed form so that you can apply it immediately.

It is our purpose to help you confront the difficult task of managing in these turbulent times. As the shape of leadership changes, The *Management Master Series* will continue to bring you the best learning available to support your own increasing artistry in the evolving science of management.

We at Productivity Press are grateful to William F. Christopher and our staff of editors who have searched out those masters with the knowledge, experience, and ability to write concisely and completely on excellence in management practice. We wish also to thank the individual volume authors; Diane Asay, project manager; Julie Zinkus, manuscript editor; Karen Jones, managing editor; Bill Stanton, design and production management; Susan Swanson, production coordination; Laser Words, text and graphics composition.

Norman Bodek
Publisher

*There is no mistake;*
*there has been no mistake;*
*and there shall be no mistake.*

— Arthur Wellesley
  Duke of Wellington (1769–1852)[1]

# 1

# INTRODUCTION

January 31, 1994, Santiago, Chile (UPI)—Chilean state copper firm Codelco is attributing a $200 million loss to bad investments in copper, gold and silver futures by one company manager. Company executive Juan Pablo Davila, 34, allegedly began speculating on the metal futures market in September after he confused sales with purchases and losses with profits—apparently due to a computer-software error. [He claimed he hit the buy key rather than the sell key on his PC, according to a PBS report.]

April 17, 1994, Anaheim, California—At Disneyland, a man falls from a Skyway gondola, landing in a tree 20 feet below. (Fortunately he suffered only minor injuries.) *The Los Angeles Times* notes that "There [was] no automatic warning device to signal an incorrectly fastened door [on the gondola]."[2]

Businesses cannot afford to make mistakes. Even if the mistakes your company makes don't make national news, they make the grapevine as customers tell their friends how you messed up. The information age only exacerbates the problem. In days gone by, unhappy customers used to tell their bad experiences to ten or twenty of their friends, by word-of-mouth, but now, by posting their experiences on electronic bulletin boards, they can reach hundreds or thousands. Even worse, the people who

1

read their postings are likely to be the very customers who are deciding whether or not to purchase your product or service. It is as if someone printed your worst mistakes in the yellow pages right alongside your ad. In such an environment, the importance of getting the defects out of the system is tantamount.

This book is about mistakes and how to prevent them from ruining your business. It's about how to rescind Murphy's Law. In this book we present a way in which you can control the mistakes that cause the defects. It allows you to go back into the process, weed out the mistakes, and ensure that they will never be a problem again. We call this *mistake-proofing.*

## WHAT IS MISTAKE-PROOFING?

Mistake-proofing is a powerful and comprehensive method for eliminating mistakes and defects, ensuring quality products and services.

### Mistake-Proofing Is Quality Control

Mistake-proofing is really quality control in its strictest sense. It does not redesign a process as reengineering does, nor does it track problems as statistical process control does. It simply keeps the system performing as it was originally designed to perform. It does this proactively, seeking out the mistakes that cause the defects and correcting them before the damage is done. You can integrate it into an ongoing TQM program or apply it independently, depending on your circumstances.[3]

### Mistake-Proofing Is a Comprehensive Method

As a method, mistake-proofing is comprehensive. You can apply it to services just as easily as to manufacturing. This is because mistake-proofing is designed to deal with defects that originate from human mistakes as well as those that originate from equipment and materials. (This is particularly important with services since they are generally more labor-intensive, and hence, more prone to human mistakes.) In addition, mistake-proofing does not require the ability to quantify some product or service attribute, only the ability to judge something as good or bad. (This is important in dealing with the largely perceptual nature of service quality.)

Most importantly, mistake-proofing is the only method we know that includes the customers' actions in the quality control system. The importance of this is emphasized by one study that estimates that customers in services are responsible for one third of the problems they complain about.[4] We do not mention this as a excuse for bad management, but rather to indicate the importance of controlling both customers' and employees' actions.

### Mistake-Proofing Is Powerful

Mistake-proofing gets results. Although the methods we present here are relatively new to services, they were adapted from an established Japanese manufacturing-based approach developed by Shigeo Shingo. The Shingo Prize is awarded to those manufacturing companies, that among other attributes, are most effective at applying his mistake-proofing techniques in the United States. Table 1 indicates the level of quality gains that some of these Shingo Prize winners attained through applying mistake-proofing.

### Mistake-Proofing Is Simple

Another big benefit of mistake-proofing is that it is simple — you don't need a Ph.D. in statistics to apply it. In reality, mistake-proofing is more like a structured form of common sense. The concepts can be easily explained,

**Table 1. Quality Gains by Selected Shingo Prize Winners**

| | | |
|---|---|---|
| **Data Corporation**<br>Minneapolis, Minnesota | • 47% reduction<br>in cost of quality | 1991 winner |
| **Glacier Vandervell Inc.**<br>Atlanta, Georgia | • 58% reduction<br>in annual scrap<br>• 54% reduction<br>in cost of quality | 1991 winner |
| **AT&T Power Systems**<br>Kansas City, Missouri | • Average outgoing<br>quality defects<br>reduced by 70%<br>• First pass yield<br>increased from 87<br>to 95% | 1992 winner |
| **Iomega Corporation**<br>Roy, Utah | • 81% reduction<br>in annual scrap<br>• 28% reduction in<br>quality costs | 1992 winner |

*SOURCE: See Note 5*

immediately applied, and there is no need to spend large amounts of money educating your employees in statistics in order to use it.

## Mistake-Proofing Is Inexpensive

Mistake-proofing is also inexpensive. Mistake-proofing devices for manufacturing usually cost under $100 and rarely exceed $500.[6] Although less widespread, the mistake-proofing devices we see in services are often inexpensive modifications to existing tools or facilities, or additions to operating software.

Mistake-proofing is also inexpensive relative to its design alternative, redundancy. Redundancy refers to having back-up resources *just in case* something goes wrong. This is obviously necessary for situations where an error can lead to a major crisis, such as a pilot having a heart attack or getting a flat tire in the desert. For most situations, however, backups are unnecessary if the system can avoid mundane errors.

## THE IDEA BEHIND MISTAKE-PROOFING

As we stated earlier, the ideas behind mistake-proofing processes were put forth by Shigeo Shingo in a system called Zero Quality Control (ZQC). Our methods build on this work, but we have generalized it so it applies to the service side of your business as well as the manufacturing side. Most notably, we have incorporated the roles of information and the customer into the framework.[7]

Mistake-proofing works on the principle that if you look behind every defect, you will find a mistake that caused it. For our purposes, we define a *mistake* as the result of an activity, either mental or physical, that deviates from what was intended. If you can correct or prevent the mistakes in your business, you will eliminate the defects. For example, a notch cut in an important machined part may be in the wrong place because the machine was not calibrated or the machinist inserted the part into the jig backwards. If you correct the mistakes by calibrating the machine and making sure the part is correctly oriented before the notch is cut, you can prevent defects. Another example is that a customer's steak may be too rare because the waiter wrote down the wrong information or the chef switched steaks with another order. To prevent the defect, make sure the waiter specifies the proper wellness before ordering and the chef places the steak with the correct order before the waiter brings it to the table.

To understand how to prevent mistakes in our businesses, we need to better understand them. Where do they come from, what causes them, how do we spot them, and how can we correct them quickly? The remaining chapters address these issues. Chapter 2 describes the main sources of mistakes in a business, the types of mistakes businesses make, and the fundamental causes behind these mistakes. Chapter 3 discusses the best places in the process to look for mistakes. Chapter 4 reports on how to detect mistakes when they occur. Chapter 5 builds on Chapter 4, introducing devices and procedures detect mistakes called *poka-yokes*. Chapter 5 also introduces the four basic types of poka-yokes and some of their most common forms; describing how they work, and illustrating them with numerous examples. Chapter 6 goes on to talk about how to design poka-yokes into your business. It also provides some general guidance on designing the mistakes out.

# 2

# SO WHERE DO MISTAKES
# COME FROM?

The sheer multitude of elements in a typical business process make the search for the source of a mistake a potentially staggering project. Fortunately, we can limit our search somewhat. If we refer back to our original definition, we remember that mistakes are deviations from intended actions. Therefore, we are concerned only with elements in the business that act upon other elements. In this manner we limit our search for mistakes to the actors in the system—people and machines. In this section we explore machine and human mistakes, the different forms they take, and the causes behind them.

## MACHINE MISTAKES

Yes, machines do make mistakes. Sometimes machines don't perform as intended due to faults of the machine itself—you might call them glitches. Some common examples of these are:

- broken tools

- empty or jammed part buffers

- miscalibration

- undetected tool wear

- mechanical failure (breakdowns)

Problems caused by the machine operator, obviously, are human mistakes, which we will discuss shortly.

Machine mistakes, being generally mechanical in nature, are better understood than human mistakes. They are, therefore, more predictable and easier to control.

If we look closely at the different types of machine mistakes, we see that they fall into two categories: those mistakes we can see coming and those that catch us unaware.

### Foreseeable Mistakes

Often a mistake shows signs that it is imminent, such as with breakdowns and tool wear. There are several well-established methods for dealing with foreseeable mistakes, which involve watching carefully for these signs, so that you can take steps to prevent the mistakes. Diagnostic monitoring methods such as vibration analysis can indicate that a machine is failing well before it becomes critical. This allows you to take it off-line and repair it during a slack period. Comprehensive maintenance programs such as total productive maintenance (TPM) can offset the effects of normal wear and tear, keeping machines in peak condition. To counter the effects of tool wear you can use tool-wear algorithms to predict the calibration adjustments that will be necessary over the lifetime of the tool. Generally, the cause of foreseeable mistakes is that tools and machines wear out as you use them.

### Unforeseeable Mistakes

Some mistakes are more problematic since there are no warning signs of an impending failure. These mistakes take the form of broken drill bits, jammed feed lines, and so on. Since there is no warning beforehand, the best we can hope for is quick detection and rapid correction of the mistake (hopefully before any damage is done). Mistake-proofing devices and methods are well suited to dealing with these contingencies. The causes behind unforseeable mistakes are also generally mechanical, but they are either less understood or simply provide no warning before failing. They therefore appear as random events.

## HUMAN MISTAKES

If we turn our attention to the mistakes that people in the system make, we quickly realize that we are discussing two very different groups of people: *employees* and *customers*. The proportion of attention you devote to these two groups varies depending on the type of business you are in. For example, a strictly manufacturing business that deals only with a limited number of corporate purchasing agents is probably less concerned with customers' effects on the system than a service business with a large amount of front-office customer interaction. Even though mistakes that corporate purchasers make can cause major operational inefficiencies, as customers, they generally know more about their role in the system and, hence, need less hand-holding.

Employees and customers interact with your business in very different ways. (Table 2 summarizes some of the major differences.) Not only do these two groups make different types of errors, but you need to treat them differently when you develop mistake-proofing devices and procedures. The types of mistakes that customers and employees make depend very much on how they experience the process.

### Employee Mistakes

Employees view the process as a series of steps that occur over and over again for each customer or product processed. As employees perform these steps, they must pay attention to three aspects of the process: the *task* or actual process steps being performed, the *treatment* of the customers, and the *tangible* aspects of the

**Table 2. How Customers and Employees Interact with Your Business**

| Employees | Customers |
|---|---|
| • Compensated for business activities | • Pay to interact with business |
| • Trained to know the appropriate steps | • Must learn steps from directions, environmental cues, prior experience, and standardized business practices |
| • Must accept responsibility for defects | • Place blame for defects |
| • Experience a continuous stream of encounters (one defect is a low failure rate) | • Experience a single encounter (one defect is total failure) |
| • Must work extra to correct defects (resulting in increased current costs) | • Dissatisfied with defects (possibly resulting in lost future revenue) |
| • Are aware of system failures, since failures slow work and require corrective effort. (Generally all failures can be completely corrected.) | • Are not aware of all system failures, but are very sensitive to those they do see. (Failures in the back office, which are corrected, never happened. Failures in the front office can never be completely corrected.) |

environment.[8] Back-office and manufacturing employees necessarily devote more attention to the actual task being performed, as they have less direct influence on the other two aspects. The types of mistakes employees make can be categorized accordingly.

- Mistakes in the *task* being performed:

  ➤ doing work incorrectly

  ➤ doing work not requested

  ➤ doing work in the wrong order

  ➤ doing work too slowly

- Mistakes in the *treatment* of the customers:

  ➤ not acknowledging the customer

➤ not listening to the customer

➤ not reacting appropriately to the customer

- Mistakes in the other *tangible* aspects of the delivery system:

  ➤ failure to clean facilities

  ➤ failure to provide clean uniforms

  ➤ failure to control noise, odors, light, and temperature

## Customer Mistakes

While employees continually cycle through the actual service encounter, customers have a more linear view of your business process. They must prepare ahead of time for their participation, engage in the encounter, and then conclude with a post-encounter resolution. The customers' mistakes can be categorized by these three stages:

- Mistakes in the *preparation* for the encounter

  ➤ failure to bring necessary materials to the encounter

  ➤ failure to understand and anticipate their role in the service transaction

  ➤ failure to engage the correct service

- Mistakes in the *encounter*

  ➤ failure to remember steps in the service process

  ➤ failure to follow system flow

  ➤ failure to specify desires sufficiently

  ➤ failure to follow instructions

## TYPES OF MISTAKES

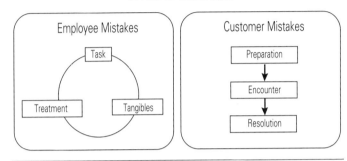

*Source: R.B. Chase, and D.M. Stewart, "Make Your Service Failsafe,"* Sloan Management Review, *Spring 1994, 35–44.*

**Figure 1. Types of Mistakes**

- Mistakes in the *resolution* to the encounter

  ➤ failure to signal service failures

  ➤ failure to learn from experience

  ➤ failure to adjust expectations appropriately

  ➤ failure to execute appropriate post-encounter actions

Figure 1 summarizes the types of human mistakes.

### The Causes of Human Mistakes

The causes behind human mistakes are more complex than those behind machine mistakes. Researchers have determined that the causes of human mistakes vary according to the level of cognitive control being used at the time. Cognitive control is the level of conscious mental processing that a person must devote to perform an activity. The three levels of cognitive control are the skill-based, rule-based, and knowledge-based cognitive control.[9]

### SKILL-BASED CAUSES

For routine tasks, such as driving a car or performing familiar manual operations, people tend to operate, more or less, on autopilot. They need very little conscious control to switch between familiar action routines according to various cues from the environment. This is *skill-based* control.

Mistakes at the skill-based level are normally due to missing a cue through inattention (such as driving past your exit ramp on the freeway while distracted by a passenger in the car), or acting on a false cue through over-attention (such as slowing to a stop because the pedestrian crosswalk signal has turned red).

### RULE-BASED CAUSES

People generally reserve the higher levels of cognitive control for problem-solving activities. When we encounter a new activity or problem, we try to match the problem with a rule or heuristic that we used successfully to solve similar problems in the past. This rule guides our actions, hopefully, to another successful conclusion. This is *rule-based* control.

Mistakes at the rule-based level of cognitive control normally involve using a good rule in the wrong situation or simply using a bad rule. For example, if a car engine turns over but won't start, a commonly applied rule is to pump the gas, which adds enough fuel to the carburetor to start the combustion in a reticent engine. However, if the engine does not start because it is flooded, then pumping the gas worsens the problem. This is an example of using a good rule in the wrong situation. On the other hand, if the car is fuel-injected rather than carbureted, then the gas should not be pumped under any circumstances. (The engine's computer determines the correct air-fuel mixture and injects the correct amount of fuel needed to start the car.) This is an example of merely using a bad rule. Choosing the wrong rule is normally the result of either insufficient or extraneous information.

### KNOWLEDGE-BASED CAUSES

If we encounter a problem for the first time, and we are sure that we have not seen anything sufficiently similar in the past, we need to use *knowledge-based* problem solving. This is where we apply pure logical deduction and symbolic manipulation, based on any relevant theory, to solve the problem. In other words, we carefully think through the problem.

Mistakes at the knowledge-based level of control usually arise because the human mind has limited processing capacity or inconsistently weighs perceptions, bases decisions on prior convictions, and makes spurious correlations in the analysis process. Anybody who has played a two-person board game such as chess, checkers, or othello understands limited processing capacity. It is relatively straightforward to examine all possible moves that can be made during your turn. With some effort, you may be able to see all of the likely responses of your opponent to each possible move. But as you try to see several moves into the future, the problem quickly becomes too large to keep in your head. We also see numerous examples of the various ways the mind weighs different stimuli. Procrastination arises because we attach greater importance to recent or upcoming events than to those that will take place in the more distant future. People who have developed a hypothesis often simply fail to see any obvious evidence contradicting it.

## Cognitive Control and Learning

Although we can learn some skills by direct observation and trial and error (e.g., learning to walk), we generally descend through this hierarchy of cognitive control as we learn. We may learn at the rule-based level, from a "cookbook" of provided rules. We may start at the knowledge-based level, carefully thinking through each step performed. In either case, as we gain familiarity, the required level of control decreases until we are operating at the skill-based level. After this initial learning period, we spend most of our time operating at the skill-based level of control. We move to higher levels of control only during those increasingly rare new situations.[10] The validity of this statement is obvious to anyone who has spent some time watching an experienced machinist or telephone sales representative perform their jobs. Even workers whose jobs require substantial thinking, such as engineers, architects, and lawyers, find they perform many aspects of their jobs by rote.

## Learning and Mistake-Proofing

The learning process has two implications for mistake-proofing. The first is that experienced employees must be treated differently from trainees because they make different mistakes for different reasons. The second applies to how you train your employees. Employees trained only at the skill- and rule-based levels of control cannot apply knowledge-based problem solving, since they lack the requisite theoretical basis. They can only apply the rules they were given or that they discovered through trial and error. Deming uses a parable about the manager who tells an employee to clean a table. The lesson is that the employee needs to know what the table will be used for to do the job right. If it is a workbench, dusting is probably just fine, but if it is an operating table, scrubbing it with alcohol is more appropriate. Similarly, if you want your employees to be able to solve problems on their own, you need to help them understand why they will be doing what you are training them to do, and how it fits into the organization as a whole. This requires knowledge-based learning.

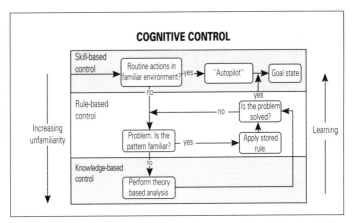

*Source: Adapted from James Reason,* Human Error *(Cambridge: Cambridge University Press, 1990), 64.*

**Figure 2. Cognitive Control**

We have looked into the types of mistakes and their causes for two reasons. First, understanding the sources of mistakes gives us a better idea of what to look for. In particular, it opens our eyes to the mistakes that customers and machines make, and the range of activities we must mistake-proof. Second, understanding the causes behind the mistakes helps us as we search for means to detect and prevent them. The flowchart in Figure 2 show how learning, mistakes, and cognitive control relate to each other.

# 3

# WHERE AND WHEN TO LOOK FOR MISTAKES

How do we go about attaining zero defects? The first trick to mistake-proofing your process is to be in the right spot at the right time to catch the mistakes. The right spot will be as close to the mistake as possible, and the right time will be all of the time.

## INSPECT CLOSE TO THE SOURCE

It is important to know *where* to look for mistakes. After detecting a mistake the information must be sent back to the point in the process where the mistake occurred so that it can be corrected. This is called *feedback.* Naturally, the slower the feedback, the greater the damage done by the mistake.

There are several reasons why slow feedback increases the damage caused by a mistake. One reason, particularly if a machine causes the mistake, is that the machine often continues to produce defects until you correct the mistake.

Another reason is what AT&T refers to as the 1-10-100 rule. "If it takes one hour for you to fix a problem on the spot, it may take ten hours to fix the problem when it is caught by someone else downstream in the organization and one hundred hours to fix when it reaches an external customer."[11] Even if only one defect results from a mistake (as is often the case with human mistakes), the damage still increases because of lost time or additional value being added to a product that has to be scrapped or reworked. For example, the defective part may soon be built into a large machine that has to be dismantled to replace it, or perhaps it will be gold-plated several steps down the line. Additionally, if feedback is slow enough, the defects may reach the customer. In "Cost of Quality" terminology, this is known as an *external failure*, which is generally considered to cost at least ten times as much as an internal failure. Not only is there the direct cost of fixing the defect, but also the damage to your reputation. Service providers are particularly susceptible to this last phenomenon, because their production and consumption are simultaneous. Defects they do not catch immediately pass directly into the hands of the customer. What is the cost to a restaurant, if a bad meal causes a customer never to return?

Feedback is made faster by moving the point where you detect the mistake closer to the point in the process where the mistake is made. As these two points become closer in space and time, the expected damage from the defect decreases to the point where you detect the mistake before it causes any defects in the first place.

## GENERAL LOCATION GUIDELINES

Shingo provides some general guidance on where to locate inspection points to minimize the feedback time. He calls these inspection points *successive checking, self-checking*, and *source inspection*.[12] We have added a fourth, *joint-inspection*, because it commonly appears in services.

**Successive checks take place immediately after a hand-off.** This means that the next person in the process inspects the work. This person can then immediately signal the problem to the person who performs the current step. Detecting the mistake here limits the number of defects to whatever is in the buffer inventory between the two steps. This form of inspection has an associated benefit: This individual must be uniquely qualified to decide on the fitness for use of the output, especially when subjective judgment is necessary. It is important to note that you do not want to use this method when the next step in the process is the hands of the customer. Having your customers check for your mistakes only leads to dissatisfied customers.

**Joint-inspection takes place during the hand-off, with both parties in the exchange inspecting the output.** [13] The most common example of this form of inspection is rereading the order to the customer to ensure correct communication. To do this effectively, it must be very easy to undo any mistakes. This is probably the maximum level of active involvement you can expect a customer to take in inspecting the work of the employees. They may be willing to take a larger role in the inspection of their own actions, however. Joint inspection is a very good method to use for information hand-offs or problems in understanding.

**Self-checking takes place before the hand-off, immediately after processing.** The employee examines the output before putting it into the queue for the next step. The feedback here is almost instantaneous, which allows the producer to correct mistakes immediately. If the mistakes can be reliably detected here, this form of inspection allows only one defective item to be produced before the mistake is corrected.

**Source inspection takes place immediately after the mistake has been made, but before it results in a defect.** In essence, we look for mistakes that we know will cause defects in the future. We correct them now so that there is no defect in the future. Other inspection methods, correctly

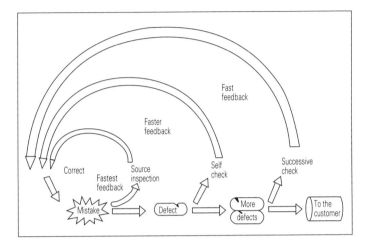

**Figure 3. Shortening the Feedback Loop**

implemented, can result in zero defects reaching the customer, but Shingo asserts that source inspection is the only way to remove all defects from the process. He cites an example in a molding-machine plant, where instead of measuring the quality defects produced, employees took great care to adjust the machines correctly before processing. Because all processing was mistake-free to begin with, they had no defects in the process to measure.[14]

## OTHER CRITICAL INSPECTION POINTS

When you locate inspection points for defects and mistakes, be sure to include the following key points:

- *Where raw material is received* — Send defective materials back to the supplier before value is added to them.
- *Prior to a costly operation* — Examples: Don't gold-plate a defective watch or start assembling an engine when the crankshaft is bent.

- *Prior to potential damage* — An off-standard part or material can cause damage in subsequent operations.

- *Prior to the point of no return* — Some materials can't be economically reworked after they go through a particular process. Examples: Typographical mistakes in books, demolishing the wrong building, cutting a diamond, and so on.

- *Prior to stocking* — Inspect work-in-process and finished goods before you stock them, especially if there is a high spoilage rate or a high cost if they are not available.

- *Where quality responsibility changes hands* — This allows tracing the source of defectives in a multi-department organization. This also pertains to situations where incentives are paid to production workers.[15]

## INSPECT ALL THE TIME

Mistakes are random events, and therefore, we must continuously watch for them. Sampling is not good enough. It looks only at a small proportion of the outputs in a process. It assumes that the rest of the outputs will be similar to the sample, and that, therefore, we can draw conclusions about the entire output, such as the total number of defects or mistakes. What it cannot tell you is that the 532nd item produced is defective (unless by chance that item happened to be in the sample). This is an important distinction, because to catch the mistakes, we need to know when we have one in front of us, not that we made 14 in the last 2000 units. What this means is that we must maintain 100 percent inspection.

All of us have heard about the futility and cost of 100 percent inspection, but the assumptions behind these claims are open to challenge. The "futility" argument assumes that there is an employee who's sole duty is inspection, and that this employee will become bored and inattentive after searching for an extended period of time. The fewer actual defects in the output, the faster the inspector's attention level will fall. Therefore, 100% inspection is unreliable and ineffective. The flaw in this argument is that it is not necessary to have an employee who's sole duty is inspection. A company can incorporate the inspection activity as a step in the work process so that the people actually making and using the items perform the inspection. In this manner, the inspectors' attention levels remain high, because the quality of the items being inspected is directly relevant to their work. Remember that early craftsmen had no trouble inspecting 100 percent of their work as they progressed.

The cost argument assumes a reasonably slow and comprehensive inspection process. There are, however, many ways to shorten the inspection process. Distributing inspection throughout the process, as suggested above, greatly reduces the burden on the worker as inspector. Each person in the process only has to remember and check a small number of parameters, because he or she is only concerned with the output of a single process step. Parameters affected during earlier steps will have already been inspected and corrected. In many cases you may not even need a formal inspection step. The correctness of the output of one step may be verified by being able to perform the operations required in the next step. Further increases in the speed of the inspection process come from the use of simple automatic inspection devices and gauges, which we will discuss in later chapters.

# 4

# FINDING THE MISTAKES

Now that we have found the right spot, how do we keep the mistakes from slipping by us? Some mistakes are easy enough to detect. Merely being in the right place at the right time is sufficient. In other cases, we may need a little help to see them when they are in front of us. Basically, the three ways in which a person can detect a mistake are through self-monitoring, detection by others, or because of some cue from the environment.[16] They vary in their effectiveness depending on the source and cause of the mistake.

## SELF-MONITORING

Self-monitoring relies on our built-in mistake detection mechanisms. At the skill-based level of control, these mechanisms operate automatically and reasonably successfully, since there is generally some visible discrepancy between the actual state and what was desired. As the level of control increases to rule-based and knowledge-based levels, this visibility is rarely there. Therefore, we must divert a more conscious effort towards looking for mistakes, and correspondingly, the success rate of detection dramatically decreases. In order for self-monitoring to detect decision mistakes, it is necessary both to know the correct outcome of the decision and to be able to see this outcome. These criteria make self-monitoring a poor choice when decisions must be right the first time, when the correct outcome is not known ahead of time, or when the result of a decision will not be apparent for a long time, if ever.[17]

As a manager, it is not necessary to worry explicitly about self-monitoring. Since it is automatic human response, you really have no control over whether people use it or not. What *is* important to know is never to rely solely on self-detection of mistakes at the rule- or knowledge-based levels of cognitive control. Self-detection of decision mistakes is very unreliable. This also applies when people are learning what will eventually be skill-based activities, since we know they must progress through the higher levels of control in the learning process.

## CHECKING BY OTHERS

Often other people can check our work for mistakes. If this second party uses the results of our work in their own, they will readily see any mistakes in it. They also have the advantage of a fresh perspective on the situation. This makes checking by others the best method to detect certain types of mistakes, particularly when objective judgment is necessary or the mistakes are in the decision-making process. Examples include faulty logic and assumptions at the knowledge-based level of cognitive control, and poor rule choices at the rule-based level.

## ENVIRONMENTAL CUES

The best way to ensure the detection of a mistake is to make sure that something in the environment makes it very obvious that one has been made. These signals from the environment are called *cues*. A good example of an environmental cue is the inevitable "extra" parts that remain after a do-it-yourself repair project. These parts make it very clear that you have not assembled the item correctly.

## Types of Cues

Clayton Lewis and Donald Norman  have compiled six types of cues a system can provide when a mistake has been made.[18] These are:

- *Warnings* — The system merely indicates that a mistake has been made, then continues with normal activity.

- *Gagging* — A mistake causes the system to grind to a halt until the mistake is cleared and the system restarted. (This is a common response in many early software programs.)

- *Nonresponse* — The system does not respond at all to a mistake; it simply does not accept input. (The cue here is not a response, but rather the absence of any.)

- *Self-correct* — The system signals that a mistake was made and suggests a similar correct response. The theory here is that you have to correct the mistake anyway, so there is no harm in having to undo a bad suggestion. A good suggestion, however, saves time.

- *Talk about it* — The system opens a dialog in order to reach an agreement about what is really intended.

- *Teach me* — (similar to "let's talk about it") — The system learns the intentions associated with the mistaken actions and delivers the intended results if these same incorrect actions are performed in the future.

These cues correspond to Shingo's warning and control methods. The first type of cue is a warning, while the remaining five are controls.[19] Control cues prevent further action until the mistake is resolved, while warning cues can be ignored. Naturally, given the choice, we would prefer some form of control cue.

### Choosing the Appropriate Cue

The exact type of cue that is most appropriate depends on the parties involved. (Remember, employees and customers see things differently.) Even though *warnings* can be ignored, everyone appreciates them. However, for people who are not intimately familiar with a process (for example, new employees and customers), *gagging* or *nonresponse* cues are particularly frustrating. These cues do not provide any information about the nature of the mistake, only an indication that one has been made.[20]

On the other hand, experienced employees, who already know why the system is gagging or not responding, do not need extraneous information and may find these cues to be very efficient. Everyone also appreciates *self-correction*. If someone developed a machine that was good at self-correcting the mistake, however, it would probably make more sense to automate the process and remove the human element altogether.

Employees who perform routine tasks probably do not want to *talk about it* with the system, but customers and trainees might find this a nice learning feature.

The last cue, *teach me*, is problematic. If the system learns too quickly, it may be confusing if people make mistakes simply because the rules keep changing. At the same time, *teach-me* cues can help the system become more user-friendly and efficient. This is a two-edged sword, so use your best judgment. The appropriateness of the cues for employees trainees and customers are summarized in the Table 3.

**Table 3. Appropriateness of the Different Cues**

|  | Employees | Trainees | Customers |
|---|---|---|---|
| Warning | √ | √ | √ |
| Gagging | √ | No | No |
| Nonresponse | √ | No | No |
| Self-Correct | ? (automate) | √ | √ |
| Let's Talk | No | √ | √ |
| Teach Me | ? | ? | ? |

This table shows that not all cues are good for every situation. It is important that the person being cued can see why the system is blocked and know how to clear it. Also, since mistake-proofing is supposed to be simple and inexpensive, the last three types of environmental cues are probably too complex to use for mistake-proofing.

## Difficulties with Environmental Cues

There are, unfortunately, two difficulties with applying environmental cues to error detection. The first difficulty is that while environmental cues are a reliable way to detect mistakes, they cannot make judgment calls, such as whether an employee was friendly, or the soup was good. With some thought, however, it is possible to approach judging quality by deciding how much of something is too much (or too little), and then using an inexpensive sensor to provide a cue at that threshold. For example, printers used to use the evenness of color to judge printing jobs, but now they use light dosimeters to ensure the color variation does not exceed a set value.

The second difficulty is providing a cue for a mistaken decision. As we mentioned before, *checking by others* can be used to detect mistakes in the decision-making process, but there are only two ways to then check the decision. The first is to know the correct answer ahead of time and compare it with your results. The problem with this in the real world is that we often don't know the correct answer ahead of time.

The second way to detect a poor decision is to compare the results with the desired outcome. Unfortunately, there is often a considerable lag time between making the decision and seeing the results. Even worse, once many decisions are made, they are irreversible. We therefore need to provide cues for a mistaken decisions rapidly and before we implement the decision on the system. Simulators are probably the best means for providing a cue under such circumstances. A good simulator allows the decision maker to quickly try out several different decisions and see the results before acting on the real system. Such simulators can be very effective at aiding decision making in large, complex systems such as refineries and nuclear power plants.

## DETECTING MACHINE MISTAKES

Detecting the mistakes that machines make is really only a variation on detecting human mistakes. Since most machines cannot detect and correct their own mistakes, their human operators must do it.[21] This leaves us with two possibilities. The first is to rely on human operators to detect mistakes. The level of mistake detection that an operation requires depends on the level of operator guidance in the process. The more complicated operations require direct and continuous control of the machine. The reliability of detecting mistakes in these situations corresponds to that of self-monitoring. Operations in which the machine is more autonomous, with the operator performing ancillary tasks such as loading and unloading require a reliability of detection that corresponds to that of detection by others.

The second, and most effective means of detection is to rely on environmental cues to signal the mistake. These are the same cues we use to indicate human mistakes.

# 5

# POKA-YOKES: DEVICES AND METHODS FOR MISTAKE-PROOF OPERATIONS

This chapter shows how to insert environmental cues into a process through the use of mistake-proofing devices or procedures. Shingo calls these devices *poka-yoke* (from the Japanese *yokeru*, "to avoid" and *poka*, "inadvertent errors"). These devices also allow us to maintain the *constant vigilance* and *inspection close to the source* that we saw was necessary to minimize the damage from mistakes in the process. Poka-yokes are:

- simple, inexpensive, therefore, cost effective.

- automatic or part of the process, therefore, always actively looking for mistakes.

- placed close to the mistake, therefore, providing feedback quickly to minimize the damage from the mistakes.

Examples of poka-yokes literally are all around us. Many common consumer products have built-in poka-yokes. For example, microwave ovens have a switch in the door as a poka-yoke to prevent running the oven with the door open. The system provides a nonresponse cue by not operating until the door is closed. Since the oven runs on a timer, you can easily forget you have left food in it.

A poka-yoke in the form of a bell or beep lets you know when your food is done. Some newer ovens continue to beep every minute or so, until you open the door, in case you missed the first warning.

The goal of this chapter is to open your eyes to the different ways you can create poka-yokes. It provides numerous examples that we hope will help you get started developing them for your own business. As you will see, you can use poka-yokes to control or prevent mistakes from machines, from employees, and even from customers. (For a tongue-in-cheek example of this refer to the Larson cartoon.)

## KEEP IT SIMPLE

Keep it simple. The key to creating mistake-proofing devices and procedures is to not do too much at once. To build a device to catch every conceivable mistake that could be produced would invariably require you to develop costly computer imaging and robotically-controlled inspection equipment. Instead, concentrate on clever, inexpensive methods to check for only one mistake at a time. If you have two possible mistakes, develop two separate devices or procedures to catch them.

Don't worry about developing an unmanageable number of devices. Remember that when checking for mistakes you are only looking for those made at the current or the previous processing step. Only a relatively small number of mistakes can occur in a given step. In addition, this number is further limited since not all possible mistakes can occur or need a special device or procedure to detect them. In essence, some mistakes, while possible, are not really conceivable. Other mistakes are so obvious they can be self-detected immediately without the help of additional cues. Toyota, which is very experienced at

**THE FAR SIDE**                    By GARY LARSON

**Figure 4. Example of a Poka-yoke**

mistake-proofing, averages about twelve devices for each machine.[22]

## TYPES OF POKA-YOKES

The numerous examples of mistake-proofing devices and procedures in both services and manufacturing are of four different types of poka-yoke: *physical poka-yokes*, *sequencing poka-yokes*, *grouping and counting poka-yokes*, and *information-enhancement poka-yokes*.[23] The names describe the methods used to sense whether or not things are as they should be. The nature of the cue (warning, gagging, etc.) can vary, but is independent of this classification.

- *Physical poka-yokes* rely on some physical property of the process. This could be a physical aspect of the product, a tool, or even a person.

- *Sequencing poka-yokes* rely on the ordering of process steps, either monitoring the correct sequence of steps, or requiring that certain mistake-prone or oft-forgotten steps be performed before continuing with more routine steps.

- *Grouping and counting poka-yokes* rely on their being a natural grouping or fixed number of items or steps, causing discrepancies to appear out of place.

- *Information enhancement poka-yokes* involve moving information across time, distance, or people in order to provide a cue that could not otherwise be detected at the removed location.

You can use these differences as a guide to facilitate the development of such devices in your own operation. Perhaps the best way to explain these methods, however, is through example. The rest of this chapter provides numerous examples of each of the four methods grouped into some of the most popular forms that each method takes.

### PHYSICAL POKA-YOKES

Physical poka-yokes identify mistakes by detecting inconsistencies among physical characteristics. These mistakes can affect size, shape, orientation, appearance, or even the presence or absence of something. We have seen at least eight common types of physical poka-yokes — those that rely on

- orientation and placement
- delimiting and controlling the physical space
- lock-outs, lock-ins, and interlocks
- go/no-go gauging
- dispensers
- detecting presence or absence
- improved visibility
- unusual physical attributes

They are not mutually exclusive, it may be possible to classify one device as more than one type of physical method). There may be other types, but these eight types serve as a starting point for developing your own physical poka-yokes.

### Orientation and Placement

There are numerous devices you can use to assure the correct orientation or placement of an item. The most common examples of these are *templates*, *jigs*, and *cutouts and guide pins*. A good example of a template is one that a certain trucking company uses. Employees consistently had trouble attaching labels at a specified distance from two sides of a container. The company introduced a poka-yoke that is a simple template employees can place over the corner of the box, leaving a window where the label is to be attached. (See Figure 5.)[24]

Another common employee mistake is positioning parts incorrectly on a machine. This can lead to defective parts and broken tools or equipment. A *jig*, such as the one shown in Figure 6, is a useful poka-yoke to prevent this. Pushing the part into the jig correctly positions it under

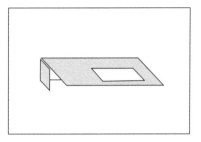

**Figure 5. Labeling Template**

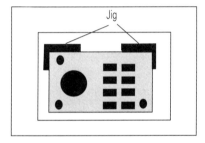

**Figure 6. Jig for Part Placement**

the working head of the machine and allows employees to drill a hole or cut a notch precisely every time.

Very often, the parts and tools that employees work with are symmetrical (or will appear so at first glance). To prevent employees from misorienting such parts during assembly or machining, they can use cutouts in the parts or guide pins attached to the parts. If the parts are not correctly oriented, the guide pins cannot fit into their respective holes, and the cutouts cannot fit over their notches. This keeps the parts from being fully inserted into the jig or the components from being attached to the assembly. (See Figure 7.) Note that in addition to the placement of the notches, different sizes or shapes for the guide pins and cutouts can help employees distinguish the correct orientation.

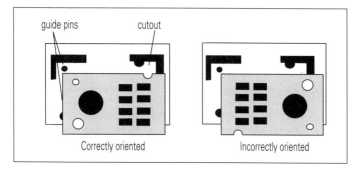

**Figure 7. Guide Pins and Cutouts (that limit orientation)**

## Controlling Physical Space

Some poka-yokes use physical constraints to control the work area. They are particularly useful for preventing mistakes where the positioning of people, rather than parts, is involved. A common mistake customers make is lying down to sleep in waiting areas, particularly in airports, and bus and train terminals. When customers lie down, they deprive other customers of seats, and detract from the appearance of the waiting area. The way to prevent this is to break up the space on the benches into areas that are too small for lying down. A good poka-yoke to accomplish this is armrests on the chairs which prevent anyone from lying down, or otherwise taking up an unfair amount of room, while at the same time giving the appearance of added luxury.[25]

The chains that configure waiting lines are another means of controlling physical space. They prevent customer mistakes by indicating where the lines should form and the number of lines to form. They also require customers to enter the end of the line to approach the serving area.

A final example of this type of poka-yoke is the common turnstile. Turnstiles function as one-way gates, allowing customer flow only in the desired direction. Turnstiles prevent customers from entering through exits, leaving through entrances, or otherwise moving against the flow.

### Lock-outs and Lock-ins

These devices provide a cue that there are special conditions for entry or exit from a space, such as the cutting area on a machine or the inside of a large mixing vat. A lock-out prevents access to an area, while a lock-in prevents exit from an area.

One effective lock-out is found in the stairwells of many older, multistory, buildings. People who visit or work in such buildings rarely use the stairs except in an emergency. During an emergency, however, unfamiliarity can cause them to circle down the stairs until they become trapped in the basement by the others behind them. In newer and renovated buildings, a separate stairway leads to the basement, but in older buildings, they may install a gate as a lock-out at the top of the last flight leading to the basement. To get to the basement, one simply opens the gate. The gate provides a warning cue in an emergency that people should leave the stairwell on this floor. Similar lock-outs can also prevent people from unintentionally entering dangerous areas in the workplace.

We can also apply lockouts to services. Lotte World theme park in Korea does not want their employees to put their hands in their pockets while standing around waiting for customers, because they feel that this does not convey the proper willingness to serve. Their simple poka-yoke to prevent this is to sew the pants pockets shut on all employee uniforms.

### Go/no-go Gauging

Go/no-go gauges are fixed gauges for quickly checking the dimensions of an item. These gauges quickly provide a cue if an item is too big (doesn't fit through a gauge) or too small (does fit through a gauge). You need two gauges (one for each tolerance limit) to tell if an item is within specifications. These gauges most often take the form of simple crossbars, fixed calipers, or circular cutouts. Similar devices can also be devised which quickly compare other physical attributes such as weight.

Gauges can be set to cue machine mistakes automatically. One such example was found in a machine that produces stem tighteners. Periodically, it produced tighteners that were too thick or thin. To detect such machine mistakes quickly, the company installed go/no-go gauges across the discharge chute from the machine. Angled across this chute are two bars mounted at different heights. They mounted the first bar at the height of the upper specification. Any tighteners that cannot fit under this bar are shunted to a side tray. They set the second bar at the lower specification limit, and any parts that fit under this bar continue to the end of the chute where they also fall into a tray. The second bar diverts all of the tighteners within specifications into a bin for accepted parts. If a tightener lands in either of the defect trays, an alarm sounds and the machine stops automatically until somebody can correct the problem. (See Figure 8.) They also adjusted the machine to decrease the likelihood of jamming, partially addressing the source of the mistake.

Such gauges are not limited to the shop floor. Customers often use such gauges to detect and prevent mistakes. Some amusement park rides require riders to be above a certain height (so they do not slip through the safety restraints) or below a certain height (to keep larger people off of rides meant only for small children). Parks do not want customers to discover they are too small or large after waiting in a potentially very long line. By placing a gauge at the front of the line, customers can tell if they are tall enough (or short enough) to go on the ride without waiting in line. (See Figure 9).

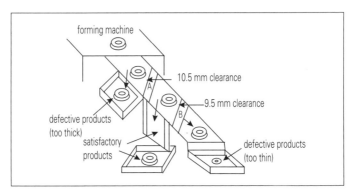

*Source:* Modern Approaches to Manufacturing Improvement: The Shingo System, *edited by Alan Robinson (Portland, Ore.: Productivity Press, 1990), 249.*

**Figure 8. Stem Tightener Go/no-go Gauging**

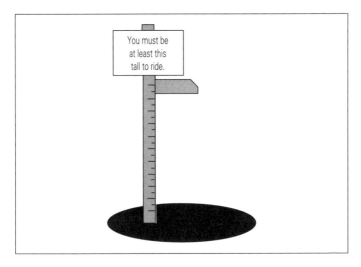

**Figure 9. Height Gauge at Amusement Park**

Another example is found at airports. Often customers discover that their carry-on luggage is too large to fit in the overhead compartments or under the seat.

This can delay the entire aircraft as the flight attendant searches for a suitable place to stow the oversize luggage. In many airports you find go/no-go gauges that are the same size and shape as the under-seat compartment placed near all check-in points (at the main desk and the gates.) Before boarding the aircraft, customers can now quickly check their carry-on luggage, to see if it fits or should be checked.

## Dispensers

Dispensers are another important physical prevention method. Generally, they release a fixed volume or mass on demand, which prevents mistakes in the measurement steps of a process. There is no cue here; these devices simply eliminate measuring mistakes. There are many simple dispensers, but our personal favorite is the McDonald's french fry scooper. McDonald's employees can make two mistakes when filling a bag of fries. If they provide too little, the customer is unhappy, but if they provide too much, McDonald's loses money. Most people have seen the McDonald's french-fry scooper — it is a simple, funnel-shaped, aluminum scoop. The employee first inserts the narrow end into the fry bag, then digs into a pile of fries with the wide end of the scoop. Once full of fries, the scoop tilts back and funnels the fries into the bag. Varying the width and length of the wide end adjusts the amount of fries gathered with the scoop to just slightly overflowing without being too generous.

## Detecting Presence or Absence

Numerous inexpensive devices can provide a cue if an item is (or is not) present at some location. These devices can warn of forgotten parts, the entry of customers, excessive (or insufficient) line-ups, or the presence of an item that is difficult to verify without assistance. For instance, attaching small limit switches to jigs, as shown in Figure 10, can turn a simple warning cue into a control (nonresponse) cue. When the part is fully pushed into the jig, it closes the switches and connects power to the machine. This eliminates mistakes because the machine will not run unless the part is fully inserted.

Simple proximity sensors cue the operator if a bit breaks on a machine. (See Figure 11.) The broken bit is too short to trigger the proximity sensor, which signals the operator with a warning light.

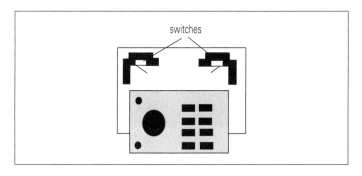

**Figure 10. Limit Switches on Jig**

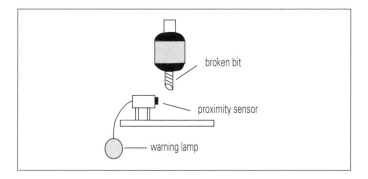

**Figure 11. Proximity Sensor Detects Broken Bit**

There are many examples of poka-yokes to detect presence or absence in services as well. Photoelectric switches operate bells on shop doors. Drive-over signals, such as bell chains at service stations, ensure that management or employees know of the customer's arrival. Line-length sensors cue to open another cash register line.

Similarly, such poka-yokes can prevent common customer resolution mistakes. For example, beepers on ATMs warn customers when they have left their card in the machine. Automatic toilets flush and automatic sinks turn off the water when the customer finishes using them.

## Improving Visibility of the Correct Choice or of the Mistake

In many cases you can make cues more visible through placement, coloration, contrast, or some other means. These poka-yokes are appropriate when a quick visual check is necessary, and a person only needs to be reminded of the appropriate activity.

At Microsoft-Ireland, workers were leaving disks in the take-up hoppers of the disk duplicating machines during customer order processing. To provide a more visible cue, the insides of the hoppers were painted white to contrast with the black diskettes.

A small manufacturer of cardboard boxes in Arizona uses a visual poka-yoke to signal when it is time to reorder cardboard stock. The company keeps the stock in stacks against a wall. They painted horizontal lines at varying heights across the wall to signal the reorder point for each type of stock. When the height of a stack gets low enough for the line to show, it is time to reorder. (See Figure 12.)

Hotels use visible cues for the housekeeping staff. They wrap paper strips around the towels, to separate the fresh towels from those that need replacement. Placing a

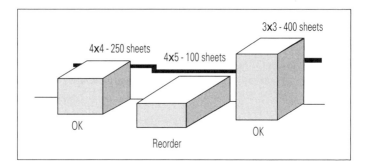

**Figure 12. Card Stock Reorder Poka-yoke**

clock next to the switchboard console can prevent operators from answering "good morning" in the afternoon.[26]

The Cleveland Medical Center uses colored lines on
the floor to help patients find their way to different areas
of the sprawling hospital. Another hospital in Indianapo-
lis color-codes the doors to patient's rooms to match the
nearby station in the hall where the patients records are
kept, making it easy for doctors to find them.

Mirrors are another common way of increasing visibility. Placing them in convenient back office locations
allows employees to inspect their personal appearance
(which affects the tangible aspects of the process). Mirrors
can also be used to decrease treatment mistakes by placing
them in front of telephone operators to ensure a "smiling
voice."

At the checkout counter, many cash registers have a
tray on top to hold the customer's payment. The visible
presence of the customer's payment reminds employees
of the denominations received and helps prevent mistakes
in making change. Additionally, many cash registers use
color-coded keys for different items to improve visibility.
Also, by folding the edges of the top two copies of a credit

card receipt to reveal the one labeled "customer copy" the customer is better able see which copy is theirs.

Taco Bell improved the visibility of the order-taking process at some of their drive-throughs by adding a display that itemizes what the customer ordered. This allows the customer to inspect the order and correct mistakes before they become defects "in the bag." Another example seen in most fast-food restaurants is the trash can with integrated tray return, which acts as a strong visual cue to customers who might not know to bus their own tables.

A final lesson in the power of improving visibility is that it works even for the very young. A child-care expert advocates placing a picture by the door of child-care centers to show children what a clean room looks like.

## Use of Unusual Physical Attributes

In some instances you can use peculiar aspects of items, such as texture, mass, or electrical properties as poka-yokes.

An excellent example of this is a device that detects and corrects upside-down washers. One company uses a machine that requires washers to be inserted with the burr side down. Noting that the smooth side slides more easily on a rough surface, an employee developed a poka-yoke out of a common belt sander, inverted and inclined as a conveyor belt. (See Figure 13.) Washers with the burr side up slide down the belt and flip over in the process. Correctly oriented washers with the burr side down are carried up the belt sander to the top where they slide down a chute.[27]

The ultimate example of a poka-yoke that uses unusual physical attributes is the coin testing unit in a vending machine. (See Figure 14.)

> The coin enters a slot, which has been carefully measured to accommodate the required coin or coins, and

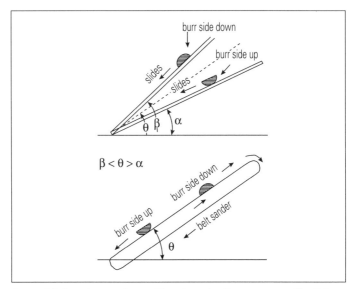

*Source:* Modern Approaches to Manufacturing Improvement: The Shingo System, *edited by Alan Robinson (Portland, Ore.: Productivity Press, 1990), 152.*

**Figure 13. Automated Sorting of Washers**

rolls down a chute to two hook-shaped balance arms. A coin of the correct weight presses the right arm sufficiently to move a counterweight on the left; displacement of the arm allows the coin to pass. The diameter of the coin is also checked at this point — too-small coins slip from the hooks to the coin return receptacle. Those that are too large get stuck. When the coin return button is pushed, a side flap opens, allowing the coin to fall into the return receptacle.

A coin of the proper size and weight continues through the machine past a strong magnetic field. If the iron content of the coin is high, for example, the magnet catches it. The coin return button triggers a wiper that sweeps the coin away from the magnet. The speed of the coin as it moves through

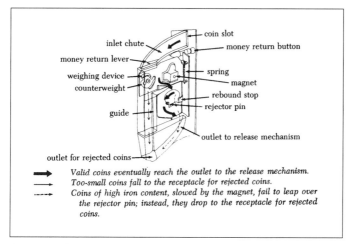

*Source: Caroline Sutton,* How Do They Do That? *(New York: Quill, 1981), 118.*

**Figure 14. Coin Testing Unit in a Vending Machine**

the machine is thus dependent on composition and mass. The speed it accumulates must be sufficient to allow the coin to jump over a rejecter pin and down an outlet leading to the release mechanism, which in turn allows the vending machine to deliver the desired product.[28]

## A Final Note of Physical Poka-Yokes

When you develop your own physical poka-yokes, do not overlook the many inexpensive electronic sensors that are available to perform almost any type of physical sensing from simple detection and proximity to thickness, vibration, and color.

### SEQUENCING POKA-YOKES

Most activities in a business consist of series of steps. Often you can use the simple fact that some steps must take place before others as part of mistake-proofing a process. Sequencing poka-yokes indicate, discourage, or prevent deviation from the order of steps in a process by making completion of a later step contingent on an earlier one. These poka-yokes often take the form of *baiting*, *task substitution*, and *interlocks*.

## Baiting

Baiting is very straightforward. It consists of a reward step to follow an often forgotten or undesirable step in a process. Receiving the reward is contingent on completing the earlier step. This is particularly useful for prompting customers to do what they otherwise wouldn't do.

The classic example of this type of poka-yoke is customer comment cards used at some hotels, which offer a free gift or rebate for filling them out and returning them to the front desk.

## Task Substitution

Task substitution is less overt than baiting. It relies on inserting steps in the process that have indirectly positive results. For example, a bank requires tellers to mark a customer's eye color on a checklist at the start of the encounter, indirectly assuring eye contact. Or, on the shop floor, a guillotine press has two separate switches that employees must push simultaneously to bring the press down. This indirectly assures the employees remove their hands from the working area.

Such poka-yokes work very well on customers. It often turns out that people who call the customer service line at a cable television company have inadvertently switched their television from channel 3 to some other channel. When asked if the television is on the correct channel, the customers may automatically say yes. To ensure that the television is tuned to the correct channel, without embarrassing the customer, the cable company has resorted to this simple poka-yoke. They ask the customer to change the channel on their television to channel 5 and back to 3 again. If the signal returns, the problem is fixed and the customer is happy. If not, the poka-yoke has eliminated at least one potential problem.

Digital Equipment Corporation (DEC) uses a similar poka-yoke. DEC asks customers to gather such information as the serial number of their system, the type of system they are using, peripheral components on the system, and the type of service plan they chose before calling the computer technical support line. Customers who wait until they are on the line with the technician to gather this information waste capacity and create longer waits for the other customers. DEC's service flier, in the form of a flowchart, acts as a task substitution poka-yoke. To determine the correct number to call, customers must answer three yes-no questions, gathering the required information in the process. (See Figure 15.)

## Interlocks

Interlocks are similar to lock-outs and lock-ins. An interlock, however, includes an additional step that removes the lock. The way interlocks prevent mistakes is much like a mechanical version of baiting, mentioned above. To accomplish the desired or easily remembered task, the person must first disengage the lock by performing the interlocking, easily forgotten or undesirable task.

An excellent place to use these poka-yokes is on machinery, that requires opertors to perform a safety task before starting the machinery. One such example is found on the machine used to balance tires. A safety hood covers the tire while it spins at high speeds to determine the

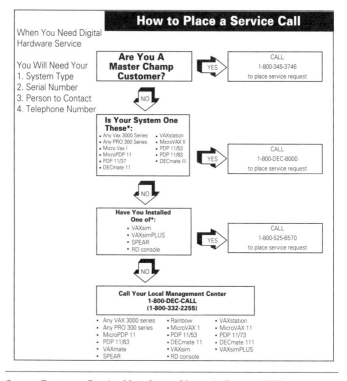

*Source:* Customer Service Newsletter, *20, no. 1, (January 1992).*

**Figure 15. Digital Equipment's Service Flyer**

correct balance. To activate the power to the machine, the operator must first close the hood.

Shingo refers to a whole host of manufacturing examples that use shuttered doors to block access to key parts until the employee takes an interlocking step, such as reaching into the oft-forgotten part bin and breaking a photo-electric beam which opens the shutters.[29]

These devices can be adapted to service uses, such as those seen on airline lavatory doors. In order to turn on the lights, the passenger must lock the door, which automatically activates the occupied sign. Another wonderful example was found in the bathrooms of L'Hotel Louis XIV. Two adjacent rooms shared each bathroom. Often, guests forgot to unlock the door that leads to the other room when they were finished. To solve this problem, the hotel removed all locks on the bathroom doors and installed an interlock poka-yoke. (See Figure 16.) It consisted of two straps that were attached to the handles of the bathroom's two opposing doors. Since the doors opened outward into the rooms, to lock the bathroom doors, the guest need only hook the straps together. To leave the bathroom, the straps had to be unhooked, "unlocking" both doors.[30]

Rubbermaid has developed a mailbox with a built-in interlocking poka-yoke. Whenever someone puts mail into the box, the flag is automatically raised, notifying the customer that mail has been delivered.

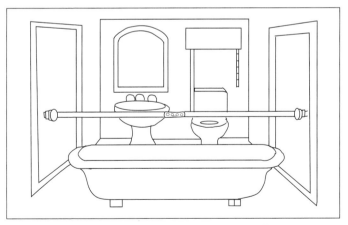

*Source: R. Caplan,* Why There Are No Locks on the Bathroom Doors in Hotel Louis XIV and Other Object Lessons *(New York: McGraw-Hill, 1984), 161.*

**Figure 16. Third-floor Bathroom in the Hotel Louis XIV**

## GROUPING AND COUNTING POKA-YOKES

Grouping and counting poka-yokes are designed to make it easier to tell when we have omitted (or included extra) objects, information, or repetitions. They are particularly useful when you deal with large numbers or set groupings. Generally these methods either do the counting for us, group many individual items into multiple-item batches (to make counting easier), or provide patterns where omissions and inclusions stand out as clear cues that something is amiss. Five of the most common types of grouping and counting poka-yokes are *counting and ordering*, *arrangement*, *kits*, *layout mats*, and *checklists*.

### Counting and Ordering

There are many inexpensive mechanical and electronic devices that can remove the burden of remembering how many times you have repeated a step, or what number you have reached in a long count. Because of the pervasiveness of these devices, we have included them as a separate category.

A manufacturer of auto bodies uses such devices on a spot welding machine. To ensure that the employees remember to make all ten welds, the company hooked up a counter to the portable spot welder and the pneumatic holding clamp. This prevents release of the clamp until the spot welder has been operated ten times. (See Figure 17.)[31]

Counters and ordering poka-yokes are common in services too. Take-a-number systems not only help prevent mistakes in serving customers out of turn, but they also free the customer from physically standing in line. Sewell Cadillac places color-coded numbered markers on cars as they arrive at the service facility.[32] The numbers assure that the customers are served in turn, and the colors signify which service advisor has responsibility for that car (an improved visibility poka-yoke).

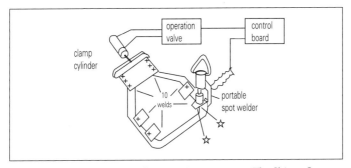

Modern Approaches to Manufacturing Improvement: The Shingo System, *edited by Alan Robinson (Portland, Ore: Productivity Press, 1990), 283.*

**Figure 17. Counter-controlled Spot Welder**

## Arrangement

Sometimes we can use the arrangement of items to facilitate our counting ability. For instance, by batching items in multiples of 10, we only have to count the batches and multiply. We can use batching with individual packages, spacing between groups, or by using a matrix with ten columns and counting the rows. A trucking company uses egg-crate-like partitions in boxes to make it clear that the correct quantity was packed.[33] In hospitals, gauze used in an operation comes packaged in fixed quantities, allowing quick determination of the number used, (to ensure that none is left in the patient). Another firm arranges their bulletin board with colors, posting messages on green, amber, and red paper for compliments, gripes, and failures respectively. A quick look at the board allows employees to assess how the company is doing.

## Kits

Kits are a quick and easy way to assure that all and only the necessary items are used. With a kit, it is impossible to use more than the number of items in the kit, and any items that remain in the kit are cues that, indicate something may have been forgotten. Manufacturers often use kits to group all of the parts needed to install a product option. This eliminates the employee having to remember which parts to retrieve and install.

In hospitals, all of the items necessary for some standard procedures, such as catheter installation, are packaged in kits. In addition to assuring both sterility and the presence of all necessary items, any unused items remaining in the kit can signal an improper installation. Some hospitals package all patient medication in the correct dosages and load them onto carts at the pharmacy. As the nurses complete their rounds, any remaining medication signals a missed patient, or changes in their treatment that need to be recorded.

### Layout Mats

Layout mats, and variations on them, rely on the principle of *a place for everything and everything in its place*. Since each item has a clearly mark place, an empty spot is a cue for an omitted item. Extra items cannot be added, because there is nowhere to put them. A layout mat confers the same benefits that a kit does. It is a particularly useful method of assembling kits from stock parts, (or reassembling them after use). Figure 18 shows a layout mat for the tools and parts necessary to hook up a television to a cable outlet.

Probably the most common place to see layout mats is on the walls of a tool room. Outlines of the tools are painted where the tools should hang, assuring that all tools are returned to their proper place, and indicating when tools are missing.

In manufacturing, layout mats are particularly useful in preparing for a machine setup. A layout mat can be used to assemble all the tools and parts necessary to take

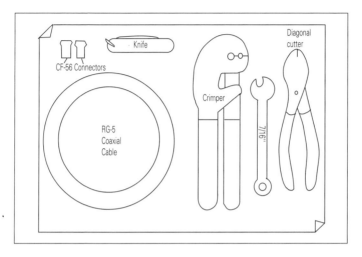

**Figure 18. Layout Mat for Hooking Television up to Cable Outlet**

a machine off-line. This eliminates running back and forth to the storage area for forgotten parts and tools while the machine stands idle.

In the operating room, surgeons use layout mats in the form of instrument trays with indentations for all of the instruments. Using these trays ensures that all of the instruments for an operation are present and sterile, and that all are removed from the patient before closing. Even child-care centers use layout mats, painting outlines for toys on the floor to indicate where they should be returned to at the end of the day.

## Checklists

Everybody is familiar with checklists — everyone uses them because they are so simple, yet effective. In fact, many pilots refer to them as being the greatest single safety device on an aircraft.

Checklists are similar to kits and layout mats, but instead of grouping physical items, they group information. This information can take the form of items to use, steps to take, or even additional information to obtain. As you meet each requirement of the checklist, you check it off or fill in the necessary information. Blank spaces on a checklist act a cues to signal missing information. A typical example is packing slips, which can be printed in the form of checklists. These allow packers to check off items as they are included.

Checklists need not be simple, itemized lists, on paper. To ensure friendliness, one fast-food company gave employees a mental checklist of four times when they should smile for maximum effect (instead of simply telling them to smile all the time). These four times were when greeting the customer, when taking their order, when asking about the dessert special, and when giving the customer change.[34] Forms are another type of checklist for gathering information, often from customers. A good form must clearly indicate what to fill out and when it is complete.

### INFORMATION ENHANCEMENT POKA-YOKES

Information enhancement poka-yokes rely on getting information to where it can be used to prevent a mistake. Often, the information is physically displaced, temporally displaced, or lost amidst all of the extraneous information people continually receive. This information can be as simple as a cue that something is wrong, or as detailed as the information necessary for decision making. Information-enhancement poka-yokes, can be high-tech and rely on telecommunications and display systems, or they can be low-tech and rely on bulletin boards and written notes. Either way they move information through time and across space or make it stand out in the flow.

## Moving Information Through Time

When we refer to moving information through time, we are really referring to three different problems, each with its own difficulties.

### STORING INFORMATION FOR LATER USE

Stored information can prevent mistakes. But this requires anticipating the information you will need and storing it where you can easily or automatically retrieve it later. We usually store information in databases and filing systems, but there are some simple, alternative means by which information for preventing mistakes can be sent into the future. Consider carrying it — wear an alarm watch to jog your memory.[35] Try mailing it — to prevent clients from forgetting appointments, mail them reminder cards.

Use the phone — send voice mail messages to yourself when you need a reminder.[36] In fact many voice mail systems allow you to record a message to send automatically to people, including yourself, at a specified time in the future. Another method, seen at computer manufacturer Gateway 2000, is to play messages on how to solve common problems to customers waiting on hold for technical support. The messages anticipate their problems and readily provide that information to them. The Gary Larson cartoon on the next page suggests another means by which you can send important information into the future.

### CONSOLIDATING INFORMATION TO GET THE BIG PICTURE

If the information is scattered over a period of time you may need to consolidate it. The most common high-tech method is to use a computerized information system (CIS). The key to success is to have well designed work screens on the system. A good work screen design consolidates the necessary information and minimizes the amount of toggling between screens. This is particularly important for customer contact people who shouldn't be

**THE FAR SIDE** By GARY LARSON

**Figure 19. Example of an Information Poka-yoke**

distracted by the information system. The PRECISION[SM] system at Rosenbluth Travel consolidates all of the information the reservationist needs. The system integrates the current planned itinerary with the customers' personal travel preferences (e.g., aisle seat), their frequent flier accounts and other bonus plans, their companies' travel policies (e.g., business class for international travel), and the reservations systems of airlines, hotels, and car rental agencies. It uses conditional logic to display this information in a cohesive format, prompting the representative with appropriate screens for each step. For instance, a layover in a city causes the screen for hotels and car rentals to appear.[37]

Although installing a new CIS can be an expensive process, changing the format and contents of the work screens on an existing or planned system is generally far simpler and less expensive. If you do it well, the changes are worth the effort.

A low-tech way of consolidating information is the bulletin board. University of Pennsylvania's food services manager gathers customer comments over time with complaint boards posted at all dining facilities. Customers can leave their comments and complaints on the boards. Over time this method compiles information on the biggest problem areas.

### PREDICTING INFORMATION

Unfortunately, we cannot see the future, so we must anticipate or forecast what the information will be. The most important forecasting method from a mistake-proofing standpoint is the simulator. The importance of simulators in detecting many decision mistakes has already been discussed in Chapter 4. Numerous readily available software packages can do anything from standard statistical forecasting to aiding the development of more subjective group predictions. The discussion of these packages, however, is beyond the scope of this book.

## Moving Information Across Space

Moving information through space is a much simpler problem than moving it through time. Modern telecommunications technologies and services now allow us to transmit information reliably over very long distances and to almost any location, reliably and inexpensively. This trend will continue, allowing richer information formats and greater speed and access, with even lower prices in the future. This does not mean that all information handling must be done electronically. At times it may still be easier or cheaper to use low-tech methods. Match the means of transmission to the richness of the information you wish to transmit. In other words, you don't need to transmit video to indicate when a customer has entered the store (a simple bell or light suffices). But, you may need video if it is important to know *who* entered the store.

One business writer advocates providing employees with a button to press, in the event of a hostile customer, that signals a manager to help resolve the problem before it gets out of hand. This allows the employee to summon the manager without leaving the customer alone and fuming.[38]

The Denver Department of Motor Vehicles complemented their take-a-number system by installing message boards, that display the current number being served, in a tavern across the street. This allows customers to play some pool and have a soft drink while waiting for their turn. The 300-seat Cove Restaurant in Deerfield Beach, Florida, issues pagers to waiting customers. This allows the customers to wander the scenic waterfront without missing their table call. The system cost about $5,000.[39] A dental office uses a similar system, issuing pagers to parents so they can shop while their child is treated.

We see two problems that arise in moving information across space and time. The first is keeping the information associated with the correct item or person as it is transmitted. Bar coding systems and ID or account cards with magnetic stripes are two readily available solutions to this problem.

The second problem is psychological. Customers are often uncomfortable when employees use computerized systems in their presence. This is partially due to the unknown, and partially due to concerns over privacy and information accuracy. A major hotel chain gets around this problem by using a low-tech system to ensure acknowledgment of a guest's repeat business. When greeting the guest, the bellman asks if this is their first stay at the hotel. If they have been a guest before, the bellman will discretely tug his ear as a signal to the front desk clerk who will greet the guest with a hearty "welcome back". Tandy Corporation's Radio Shack stores address this problem more directly. When clerks enter customer information, they turn the screen so that the customer can also see what is there. This allows the customer to check the accuracy of the current information.[40]

## Making Information Stand Out

Sometimes we lose track of certain information in the endless stream of information that immerses us. Maybe we have to sort through too much irrelevant stimuli, or maybe the cue is simply too weak. What we need in these instances is to make the information stand out against the background much like we did with the physical poka-yokes for improving visibility. The methods for doing this make the subtle cues more obvious. Strategically placed microphones can ensure that customers' and servers' voices are audible. In some restaurants waitresses put doilies under the cups with decaffeinated coffee so they can differentiate them from the regular coffee when refilling. Cues such as badges, gold braid, and trainee buttons help convey information needed to identify different roles.

Sometimes the best recourse is to be blunt. Dress code requests on invitations can clarify a potentially vague standard. To prevent customers from explaining their problems to someone who routes calls, switchboard operators can answer the phone "Good morning, ABC Company. How (or where) may I direct your call?"[41]

A final option is to increase peoples' sensitivity, so they can detect subtle cues. Many service companies train their employees to read negative nonverbal cues in their customers to prevent miscommunication from escalating into a complete service failure.

# 6

## DESIGNING OUT THE MISTAKES

There are two ways of implementing mistake-proofing in your organization. The first is to jump right in and start mistake-proofing any problems you see. This gets your feet wet and builds confidence in mistake-proofing. We do not recommend it as an ongoing methodology, however. If you want to obtain more substantial mistake-proofing gains, we suggest mapping out the system to guide you in placing mistake-proofing devices where they do the most good. Place the devices as close to the original mistake as possible and where they correct the biggest problems facing your organization first. In this section, we briefly discuss how to map your process, and how to locate mistake-proofing devices in the context of an example from an automotive service facility. We conclude by providing some guidelines for developing you own poka-yokes and discussing some more general design issues.

### PROCESS MAPS

Process maps (or blueprints, as they are sometimes known) provide us with a means of integrating steps in a process with the information and people involved. The process maps we discuss here were originally developed by Lynn Shostack for use in designing services.[42] They are basically enhanced process flowcharts that incorporate additional information such as people involved, points of interaction, means of contact, and flow of information.

Constructing a process map is relatively straightforward, though potentially time-consuming, depending on the size of the process and the level of detail included. Following are some guidelines for constructing process maps.

### Guidelines for Mapping a Process

1. List process steps chronologically from left to right on the page.

2. Vertically arrange participants in the process from top to bottom, with the customers at the top, the employees (ranging from the front line to the most removed) in the middle, and the support systems and suppliers along the bottom.

3. Record the steps in the process horizontally according to time and vertically according to the participant who performs the step. As with flowcharting, you can use different shapes to differentiate between activities, for example, diamonds for decisions, triangles for waiting, and boxes for processing.

4. Draw lines to connect the process steps. (Use different styles to indicate the flow of materials, people, and information.)

5. Draw lines of interaction between all of the participants. (These are horizontal lines that run across the page, separating the steps that each participant does.) A hand-off occurs between two participants where the process lines cross the lines of interaction. By the type of line we can tell what was handed off. This information is useful to us since so many mistakes occur during or because of hand-offs.

6. The final step to complete the process map is to draw a line that separates the steps that are visible to the customer from those that occur behind the scenes. This is the line of visibility. If you are a manufacturer, very little of your process may be visible to the customer. On the other hand, it is possible that almost all of the steps in a service may be visible to its customers. Earlier, when we discussed the differences between customers and employees, we mentioned that you can correct the mistakes the customer cannot see with little damage to the perceptions of your organization (although the correction may still be financially costly). It is much more important to prevent the mistakes that customers can see, before they damage your reputation.[43]

## Using the Process Map

After completing the process map, you can use it to guide the introduction of mistake-proofing devices into your organization as follows:

1. Determine what are the most serious mistakes.

2. Locate where they have been detected on the process map.

3. Trace back along the process lines to find the original source of the mistake. Look for mistakes from any of the sources: *employees* (in *task*, *treatment*, or *tangibles*), *customers* (in *preparation*, *encounter*, and *resolution*) and *machines*. Make sure you trace back far enough. The first participant in the process may appear to be the source, but it may be necessary to look a little further back to find the actual source. The employee you finger as the source of defective parts may be working on a miscalibrated machine,

Failure: Customer forgets the need for service. Poka-yoke: Send automatic reminders with a 5 percent discount.

Failure: Customer can not find service area, or does not follow proper flow. Poka-yoke: Clear and informative signage directing customers.

Failure: Customer has difficulty communicating problem. Poka-yoke: Joint inspection- service advisor repeats his/her understanding of the problem for confirmation or elaboration by the customer.

Failure: Customer does not understan the necessary service. Poka-yoke: Pre-printed material for most services, detailing work, reasons, and possibly a graphic representation.

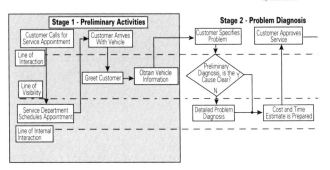

Failure: Customer arrival unnoticed. Poka-yoke: Use a bell chain to signal arrivals.

Failure: Customers not served in order of arrival. Poka-yoke: Place numbered markers on cars as they arrive. Failure: Vehicle information incorrect and process is time consuming. Poka-yoke: Maintain customer database and print forms with historical information.

Failure: Incorrect diagnosis of the problem. Poka-yoke: High-tech check lists such as expert systems and diagnostic equipment.

Failure: Incorrect estimate. Poka-yoke: Check lists itemizing costs by common repair types.

*Source: R.B. Chase, and D.M. Stewart, "Make Your Service Failsafe,"* Sloan Management Review, *Spring 1994, 35–44.*

**Figure 20. Mistake-proofing a Typical Automotive Service Operation**

Failure: Customer not located.
Poka-yoke: Issue beepers
to customers who wish to
leave facility.

Failure: Bill is illegible.
Poka-yoke: Top copy to
customer, or plain
paper bill.

Failure: Feedback not obtained.
Poka-yoke: Customer
satisfaction postcard given to
customer with keys to
vehicle.

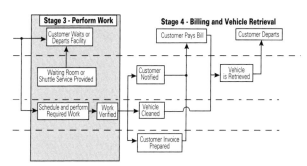

Failure: Service shuttle is
inconvenient
Poka-yoke: Seating in
available shuttles is
allocated when
scheduling appointments.
Lack of free spaces indicates
that customers needing
shuttle service should be
scheduled for another
time.
Failure: Parts are not in
stock.
Poka-yoke: Limit switches
activate signal lamps when
part level falls below order point.

Failure: Vehicle not cleaned
correctly.
Poka-yoke: Person retrieving
vehicle inspects, orders a touch-up
if necessary, and removes floor
mat in presence of customer.

Failure: Vehicle takes too long
to arrive.
Poka-yoke: When cashier enters
customer's name in order to print
the bill, information is electronically
sent to runners who retrieve
vehicle while the customer is
paying.

which in turn may be the result of faulty calibration equipment.

4. Determine the cause of the mistake.

5. Develop an appropriate poka-yoke, locating it as close as possible to the source of the mistake. Preferably, the poka-yoke should provide a controlling cue, but remember to be sensitive to *who* is being mistake-proofed.

Figure 20 shows a simplified blueprint of a typical automotive repair operation. It shows some of the common mistakes and suggests poka-yokes to prevent them.

## DEVELOPING MISTAKE-PROOFING DEVICES OR PROCEDURES

We have little advice to offer on the subject of designing your own poka-yokes. Unfortunately, not much science is involved — the process is more one of brainstorming possibilities. We can only offer you the following limited guidelines:

1. Start by examining the cause of the mistake and its physical, informational, and procedural surroundings to see which type of poka-yoke (Chapter 5 discusses types of poka-yokes) is appropriate.

2. Brainstorm with a team, preferably one that is actively involved in the process. This is not absolutely necessary, but as with any brainstorming activity, a group can provide synergistic effects and, hence, produce more potential solutions.

3. Mistake-proof only one mistake at a time. (Remember that Toyota uses, on average, 12 devices per machine.)

4. Remember that the goal is to develop clever, simple, and inexpensive devices. (Don't immediately opt for the high-tech solution.)

5. Look through the examples of each type of poka-yoke as a means of inspiring the imagination.[44]

6. Apply Shingo's 50-50 rule: If you are 50 percent sure that a device will work, try it out. If it fails, you will probably learn enough in the process to build a second one that does work.[45]

A final note on the subject of developing poka-yokes: When all else fails, remember, it still may be possible to introduce brute automation and redundancy to detect and correct mistakes. Automated inspection can often be relatively inexpensive if computers are already heavily involved in the process. A good example of this is found with the latest version of Microsoft's word processor, Word®, which can be configured to continuously check and correct typographical mistakes as you work. In instances where the mistakes may be highly subjective or the work highly abstract, it may be necessary to have a redundant inspection. Many consulting firms often have a second "peer review" of all reports by another consultant. A similar system exists in the legal department of Motorola, which employs the "two-lawyer rule": a second in-house lawyer reviews all contracts to check for mistakes.[46]

## OTHER IMPORTANT DESIGN ISSUES

You may find certain other concepts interesting when you design your processes to prevent mistakes. These are particularly relevant for customers, because they are less familiar with the peculiar workings of your process.

### Visibility

The first concept is that of *visibility*. Many times we can determine the correct operation of a physical device by getting cues about how it works. For example, we know that doors swing around the hinges. Therefore, if the hinges are visible, we know which side of the door to push. Other devices on the door, such as push plates, can also indicate where to push and even whether to push or pull.

### Real-world Mapping

Another related concept is the idea of real-world mapping. This kind of mapping connects controls with what they control. As a result, we are able to use our pre-existing knowledge of the system to determine how to manipulate the controls to achieve our desired result.

Anybody faced with a bank of switches that bear no relation to the lights or equipment they operate understands the benefits of real-world mapping. Imagine you are in a room with three banks of lights, one across the front of the room, one across the middle, and the last across the rear. If the three switches that control these lights are mounted, side-by-side, on the front wall, it is unclear which switch controls which bank of lights. If, instead, the switches are mounted on the side wall, it is easy to tell that the switch closest to the front of the room controls the front bank, the middle switch controls the middle bank, and the switch closest to the rear of the room the rear bank of lights. The switches are mapped onto the real world.

### Standards

Where visibility and real-world mapping cannot be applied, it may be possible to use some widely accepted standards to ease operation. Instead of learning an arbitrary configuration or procedure, use standards that require you only to draw the connection between the current situation and the situation to which the standards apply, and then use the already known standards. There are many such standards to draw on, for example, open into rooms from the hallway, hot water is on the left, valves turn clockwise to shut, press "F1" for help, and move switches up for on.

The complexity and broad applicability of some standards is simply remarkable. Roger Shank, a noted cognitive scientist, relates this story about using a standardized restaurant script while traveling through a small town in Israel.

> I know no Hebrew, and the owner of the only restaurant in town spoke no language that I knew. I walked in, looked at the owner inquiringly, established that we had no language in common, and then we stared at each other for a while. He began to motion towards his mouth. I took this as a question about whether I had come into this establishment to eat, so I nodded, and he showed me a table. The menus were in Hebrew, so I was lost. The owner asked me some questions and upon realizing that this method was not going to work, went into the kitchen. He came back holding a dead chicken by the neck. He showed it to me. I took this to be a question about whether I wanted chicken. … I nodded okay. Sometime later, I was served broiled chicken, and I paid the check and left.[47]

Schank and the proprietor were able to complete a business transaction without any form of higher communication simply because both knew and agreed upon the standard script.

Just as using a standard process can help prevent customer mistakes, working against a strong standard can cause mistakes. Think of the confusion generated when you go to the only gas station in the area that wants you to pump first, then pay. You end up walking to the cashier twice, the first time to be told "go ahead and pump it", and the second to pay for the gas. When your business operates against standards, it is very important that you take extra precautions (including the use of poka-yokes) to prevent customers from becoming confused. A good poka-yoke for the gas station would be to prominently place easily read signs in strategic places, such as on the pump handle and over the cashier window. The "pump first" stickers that most gas stations use are ineffective. They are too small and are usually lost amidst the clutter of other stickers on the pumps or on nearby support columns where the customer does not regularly look.

# 7

## SUMMARY

To get full benefit from mistake-proofing, it is important to understand where it works best, its effect on your customers, and its impact on your employees' jobs.

### MISTAKE-PROOFING WORKS BEST WHEN...

**1. There is a fixed sequence of operations that are routinely followed.** Ideally these should be linked in order to form an obvious value-added chain of activities.

**2. Each operation has clearly identifiable goals and specifications.** If you don't know what you want in the way of system outcomes at each step, you should spend time rethinking the design, rather than mistake-proofing.

**3. The number and range of inputs you must control for each operation is small.** While one of the big advantages of poka-yokes is controlling multiple inputs, simple systems are inherently easier to mistake-proof.

**4. The customer "knows the drill" in general terms, at least.** The more familiar the customer is with the process, the less you have to explain it, and the fewer the number of contingencies you have to mistake-proof.

**5. Tasks and tangibles rather than treatments are the core features of the service.** It's simply easier to set poka-yokes for actions rather than attitudes. But remember, you can mistake-proof even treatments to some degree.

**6. The process design must be fundamentally sound.** Motivating employees to mistake-proof a rational process is a lot easier than motivating them to mistake-proof a flaky one.

## MISTAKE-PROOFING AND YOUR CUSTOMERS

Customers appreciate dealing with businesses that run in a business-like fashion, that is, that don't make mistakes. By and large they are willing to follow procedures to assure that the organization meets this objective. The key is to make clear through work and deed that mistake-proofing is to their direct benefit, not just some way to make life easy for the company.

## MISTAKE-PROOFING AND YOUR EMPLOYEES

Does mistake-proofing limit employee discretion? Absolutely. If the worker must follow a checklist, act on specific warning cues, or is constrained by a mechanical device to put a part in the machine just so, discretion is eliminated. On the other hand, if such methods free up the employee's mind to deal with decisions that require some creativity, their job is both simplified and enriched. The point is that mistake-proofing is analogous to automation—it works best for all when the dull and risky portions of it are under system control, and the challenging and interesting parts are in the hands of the employee.

## HOW FAR CAN YOU GO IN MISTAKE-PROOFING?

We know that even the most aggressive mistake-proofing is still subject to Murphy's Law. Nevertheless, you can keep this to a minimum if you are creative and dedicated in your mistake-proofing efforts.

Go out and start mistake-proofing![48]

# NOTES

## Chapter 1

1. *Bartlett's Familiar Quotations* (Little, Brown and Company, 1980).

2. "Man Falls from Disneyland Ride" *The Los Angeles Times*, 18 April 1984, sec. B, p.1.

3. Mistake-proofing often replaces SPC in TQM programs. Many times, SPC is adopted in order to control the number of defects being produced by the system. In reality, SPC is a system for tracking and monitoring deviations or defects. Although this information is useful in evaluating the effects of process or material changes, SPC, in itself, does nothing to control the number of defects being produced. In addition, SPC control charts are actually designed to ignore a certain number of defects as part of the common-cause variation. Mistake-proofing, however, is designed to both *detect and correct all defects*.

4. Kristin Anderson and Ron Zemke, *Delivering Knock Your Socks Off Service* (New York: AMACOM, 1991): 39–40.

5. These statistics are excerpted from recipient profiles of the Shingo Prize. These profiles and guidelines for applying for the award can be obtained from The Shingo Prize, College of Business, Utah State University, Logan, UT 84322–3521.

6. Based on costs reported in Shigeo Shingo, *Zero Quality Control: Source Inspection and the Poka-yoke System* (Portland, Ore.: Productivity Press, 1986), 139–261.

7. Although this text is more heavily grounded in error theory, those readers familiar with Shingo's work should feel comfortable with this new framework. The most noticable changes will be to his classification scheme. We have been forced to make modifications to generalize it for services,

since many of the mistake-proofing devices that we see in services simply do not fit well into Shingo's classifications.

## Chapter 2

8. R.B. Chase and D.M. Stewart, "Failsafe Services," in *The Service Quality Handbook*, edited by E. Scheuing and W. Christopher (New York: AMACOM, 1993), 347–357.

9. James Reason, *Human Error* (Cambridge: Cambridge University Press, 1990).

10. Jens Rassmussen, "Mental Models and the Control of Action in Complex Environments," in *Mental Models and Human-Computer Interaction 1*," edited by D. Ackermann and M.J. Tauber (North Holland: Elsevier Science Publishers B.V.), 41–69.

## Chapter 3

11. AT&T Quality Steering Committee, *Sharing the Quality Vision* (Burlington, Mass.: Organizational Dynamics, Inc., 1989), ix.

12. Shigeo Shingo, *Zero Quality Control: Source Inspection and the Poka-yoke System* (Portland, Ore.: Productivity Press, 1986).

13. Chase and Stewart, op. cit.

14. Shingo, op. cit, 51.

15. D.R. Tansik, R. Chase, and N. Aquilano, *Management: A Life Cycle Approach* (Homewood, Ill.: Irwin, 1980). 368.

## Chapter 4

16. James Reason, *Human Error* (Cambridge: Cambridge University Press, 1990), 149.

17. Ibid.

18. C. Lewis and D. Norman, "Designing for Error" in *User-Centered System Design*, edited by D. Norman and S.W. Draper (Hillsdale, N.J.: Lawrence Erlbaum Associates, Publishers, 1986), pp. 411–432.

19. Shigeo Shingo, *Zero Quality Control: Source Inspection and the Poka-yoke System* (Portland, Ore.: Productivity Press, 1986), 91–101.

20. It is interesting to note that many people find a "non-response" cue to be a challenge to overcome or work around. If a detection method causes people to work around the problem, it will not be of very much use.

21. The possible exception could be advanced computer automated machinery, but the nature of such equipment is such that the mistake-detection capability must be built in by the designers and, hence, will not be under the influence of the typical manager.

## Chapter 5

22. A.G. Robinson and D.M. Schroeder, "The Limited Role of Statistical Quality Control in a Zero Defect Environment," *Production and Inventory Management Journal* 31 (1990): 60–65.

23. The first three correspond roughly to Shingo's classifications of "contact," "sequence," and "fixed value" methods. The fourth was added to incorporate many of the service poka-yokes that simply did not fit into Shingo's framework.

24. Richard J. Schonberger and Edward Knod, *Operations Management: Improving Customer Service*, 5th edition (Burr Ridge, Ill.: Irwin, 1994), 106.

25. Numerous other examples of clever designs to prevent people from lying on the benches can be found at many city bus stops, but unlike armrests, few have positive connotations associated with them.

26. Stephen Broydrick, *How May I Help You? Providing Personal Service in an Impersonal World* (Burr Ridge, Ill.: Irwin, 1994), 24.

27. Ibid.

28. Ibid.

29. Shigeo, Shingo, *Zero Quality Control: Source Inspection and the Poka-yoke System* (Portland, Ore.: Productivity Press, 1986).

30. R. Caplan, *Why There Are No Locks on the Bathroom Doors in Hotel Louis XIV and Other Object Lessons* (New York: McGraw-Hill, 1984): 161.

31. Alan Robinson, *Modern Approaches to Manufacturing Improvement: The Shingo System* (Portland, Ore.: Productivity Press, 1990), 283.

32. C. Sewell and P.B. Brown, *Customers for Life* (New York: Doubleday, 1990).

33. Schonberger and Knod, op. cit. 106.

34. F. Luhans and T. Davis, "Applying Behavioral Management Techniques in Service Organizations," in *Service Management Effectiveness*, edited by D. Bowen et al. (San Francisco: Jossey-Bass, 1990), 177–209.

35. Stephen Broydrick, *How May I Help You? Providing Personal Service in an Impersonal World*, 85.

36. Ibid.

37. Hal Rosenbluth and Diane McFerrin Peters, *The Customer Comes Second and Other Secrets of Exceptional Service* (New York: Quill, 1992), 96.

38. Clay Carr, *Front-Line Customer Service: 15 Keys to Customer Satisfaction* (New York: John Wiley and Sons, 1990), 118.

39. J. Edelson, "The Food Service Industry: Examples in Products and Services" (Los Angeles: University of Southern California, Failsafe Project Report, June 1989.)

40. Stephen Broydrick, op. cit. 33.

41. Ibid, 24.

## Chapter 6

42. Lynn G. Shostack, "Designing Services that Deliver" *Harvard Business Review* 62, no. 1 (January-February 1984), 133–139.

43. Those readers who are interested in more detail on creating process maps are referred to Jane Kingman-Brundage, "The ABCs of Service System Blueprinting" in *Designing a Winning Service Strategy*, edited by M.J. Bittner and L.A. Crosby (Chicago: American Marketing Association, 1989).

44. For those in need of more inspiration, many more manufacturing examples can be found in Shigeo Shingo, *Zero Quality Control: Source Inspection and the Poka-yoke System* (Portland, Ore.: Productivity Press, 1986), and *Poka-Yoke: Improving Product Quality by Preventing Defects*, edited by Nikkan Kogyo Shimbun/Factory Magazine (Portland, Ore.: Productivity Press, 1988.)

45. Shigeo Shingo, op. cit.

46. R.E. Yates, "Lawyers not Exempt for Quality Crusade," *Recrafting America* (Chicago: Chicago Tribune Company, 1991.)

47. Roger C. Schank, *The Connoisseur's Guide to the Mind* (New York: Summit Books, 1991), 86.

48. Let us know of any mistake-proofing ideas you have run across or developed. We will acknowledge your contribution for those used in subsequent editions of this book.

## ABOUT THE AUTHORS

**Richard B. Chase** is Justin B. Dart Term Professor of Operations Management and Director of the Center for Operations Management Education and Research at the School of Business Administration, University of Southern California.

He has taught at the Harvard Business School, IMD, and the University of Arizona. His research examines service strategy, service quality, and value-added service in manufacturing. He is the coauthor of a leading textbook in operations management and has published articles on service systems in such journals as the *Management Science*, *Decision Sciences*, and *Operations Research*. His *Harvard Business Review* article,"Where Does the Customer Fit in a Service Operation?" has been cited as a classic in the field. He is a Fellow of the Academy of Management and the Decision Sciences institute, and was an Examiner for the Malcolm Baldrige National Quality Award.

**Douglas M. Stewart** is a Ph.D. Candidate in Information and Operations Management at the School of Business Administration, University of Southern California. He also works for the Center for Operations Management Education and Research on projects relating to services and quality management. His research focuses on the design of robust service systems. He has published several papers on the topic of mistake-proofing services, and lectured on the subject to both academics and business professionals. Mr. Stewart holds a M.S. in Management and a B.S. in Mechanical Engineering, both from North Carolina State University.

# The Management Master Series

The *Management Master Series* offers business managers leading-edge information on the best contemporary management practices. Written by highly respected authorities, each short "briefcase book" addresses a specific topic in a concise, to-the-point presentation, using both text and illustrations. These are ideal books for busy managers who want to get the whole message quickly.

## Set 1 — Great Management Ideas

1. *Management Alert: Don't Reform—Transform!*

   Michael J. Kami

   Transform your corporation: adapt faster, be more productive, perform better.

2. *Vision, Mission, Total Quality: Leadership Tools for Turbulent Times*

   William F. Christopher

   Build your vision and mission to achieve world class goals.

3. *The Power of Strategic Partnering*

   Eberhard E. Scheuing

   Take advantage of the strengths in your customer-supplier chain.

4. *New Performance Measures*

   Brian H. Maskell

   Measure service, quality, and flexibility with methods that address your customers' needs.

5. *Motivating Superior Performance*

   Saul W. Gellerman

   Use these key factors—nonmonetary as well as monetary—to improve employee performance.

6. *Doing and Rewarding: Inside a High-Performance Organization*

   Carl G. Thor

   Design systems to reward superior performance and encourage productivity.

PRODUCTIVITY PRESS, Dept. BK, PO Box 13390, Portland, OR 97213-0390
Phone (503) 235-0600                    Fax (503) 235-0909

**Set 2 — Total Quality**

7.  *The 16-Point Strategy for Productivity and Total Quality*
    William F. Christopher and Carl G. Thor
    Essential points you need to know to improve the performance of your organization.

8.  *The TQM Paradigm: Key Ideas That Make It Work*
    Derm Barrett
    Get a firm grasp of the world-changing ideas behind the Total Quality movement.

9.  *Process Management: A Systems Approach to Total Quality*
    Eugene H. Melan
    Learn how a business process orientation will clarify and streamline your organization's capabilities.

10. *Practical Benchmarking for Mutual Improvement*
    Carl G. Thor
    Discover a down-to-earth approach to benchmarking and building useful partnerships for quality.

11. *Mistake-Proofing: Designing Errors Out*
    Richard B. Chase and Douglas M. Stewart
    Learn how to eliminate errors and defects at the source with inexpensive poka-yoke devices and staff creativity.

12. *Communicating, Training, and Developing for Quality Performance*
    Saul W. Gellerman
    Gain quick expertise in communication and employee development basics.

These books are sold in sets. Each set is $85.00 plus $5.00 shipping and handling. Future sets will cover such topics as Customer Service, Leadership, and Innovation. For complete details, call 800-394-6868 or fax 800-394-6286.

PRODUCTIVITY PRESS, Dept. BK, PO Box 13390, Portland, OR 97213-0390
Phone (503) 235-0600                                     Fax (503) 235-0909

## BOOKS FROM PRODUCTIVITY PRESS

Productivity Press provides individuals and companies with materials they need to achieve excellence in quality, productivity, and the creative involvement of all employees. Through sets of learning tools and techniques, Productivity supports continuous improvement as a vision, and as a strategy. Many of our leading-edge products are direct source materials translated into English for the first time from industrial leaders around the world. Call toll-free 1-800-394-6868 for our free catalog.

### Poka-yoke
#### Improving Product Quality by Preventing Defects
*Nikkan Kogyo Shimbun Ltd. and Factory Magazine (ed.)*
If your goal is 100 percent zero defects, here is the book for you—a completely illustrated guide to poka-yoke (mistake-proofing) for supervisors and shop-floor workers. Many poka-yoke devices come from line workers and are implemented with the help of engineering staff. the result is better product quality—and greater participation by workers in efforts to improve your processes, your products, and your company as a whole.
ISBN 1-915299-31-3 / 295 pages / $65.00 / Order IPOKA-B246

### Zero Quality Control
#### Source Inspection and the Poka-yoke System
*Shigeo Shingo*
Dr. Shingo reveals his unique defect prevention system, which combines source inspection and poka-yoke (mistake-proofing) devices that provide instant feedback on errors before they can become defects. The result: 100 percent inspection that eliminates the need for SQC and produces defect-free products without fail. Includes 112 examples, most costing under $100. Two-part AV program also available; call for details.
ISBN 1-915299-07-0 / 328 pages / $75.00 / Order ZQC-B246

### Companywide Quality Management
*Alberto Galgano*
Companywide quality management (CWQM) leads to dramatic changes in management values and priorities, company culture, management of company operations, management and decision-making processes, techniques and methods used by employees, and more. Much has been written on this subject, but Galgano—a leading European consultant who studied with leaders of the Japanese quality movement—offers hands-on, stage-front knowledge of the monumental changes CWQC can bring.
ISBN 1-56327-038-2 / 480 pages / $45.00 / Order CWQM-B246

PRODUCTIVITY PRESS, Dept. BK, PO Box 13390, Portland, OR 97213-0390
Phone (503) 235-0600                    Fax (503) 235-0909

**A New American TQM**
**Four Practical Revolutions in Management**
*Shoji Shiba, Alan Graham, and David Walden*
For TQM to succeed in America, you need to create an American-style
"learning organization" with the full commitment and understanding of
senior managers and executives. Written expressly for this audience, *A
New American TQM* offers a comprehensive and detailed explanation of
TQM and how to implement it, based on courses taught at MIT's Sloan
School of Management and the Center for Quality Management, a con-
sortium of American companies. Full of case studies and amply
illustrated, the book examines major quality tools and how they are being
used by the most progressive American companies today.
ISBN 1-56327-032-3 / 606 pages / $50.00 / Order NATQM-B246

TO ORDER: Write, phone, or fax Productivity Press, Dept. BK, P.O. Box
13390, Portland, OR 97213-0390, phone 1-800-394-6868, fax 1-800-
394-6286. Send check or charge to your credit card (American Express,
Visa, MasterCard accepted).

U.S. ORDERS: Add $5 shipping for first book, $2 each additional for
UPS surface delivery. We offer attractive quantity discounts for bulk
purchases of individual titles; call for more information.

INTERNATIONAL ORDERS: Write, phone, or fax for quote and indicate
shipping method desired. For international callers, telephone number is
503-235-0600 and fax number is 503-235-0909. Prepayment in U.S.
dollars must accompany your order (checks must be drawn on U.S.
banks). When quote is returned with payment, your order will be shipped
promptly by the method requested.

NOTE: Prices are in U.S. dollars and are subject to change without notice.

PRODUCTIVITY PRESS, Dept. BK, PO Box 13390, Portland, OR 97213-0390
Phone (503) 235-0600                    Fax (503) 235-0909